STIFTUNG
PREUSSISCHE SCHLÖSSER UND GÄRTEN
BERLIN-BRANDENBURG

Harald Berndt · Jörg Kirschstein

Schloss Cecilienhof

Tudor Romanticism and World Politics

in collaboration with
Bärbel Stranka

Prestel

Munich · Berlin · London · New York

CONTENTS

Schloss Cecilienhof as the Residence of Crown Prince William and his Family

Between 1913 and 1917, Kaiser William II (1859–1941) had Schloss Cecilienhof built in the north-eastern end of the Neuer Garten (New Garden) for his oldest son, Crown Prince William (1882–1951), and his wife, Duchess Cecilia zu Mecklenburg (1886–1954). The spacious country house consisted of 176 rooms and was equipped with the most modern comforts of the time. Central heating even permitted this last castle to be built by the Hohenzollern to be lived in during winter. After their wedding in 1905, the Crown Prince and his wife lived in the neighbouring Marmorpalais (Marble Palace). The classicistic building has an idyllic location on the banks of the Heilige See (Sacred Lake) and had been previously lavishly renovated. In spite of this, two years after their marriage, the decision was taken to build a new castle for the successor and his wife. Excavation work began next to Schloss Babelsberg in 1908. The plans for the extension were so gigantic that they would have made Schinkel's original building seem completely insignificant. At the end of 1908, the Chancellor of the Reich, Prince Bülow, proclaimed a financial reform calling on all citizens to be extremely thrifty. Following this, construction of the extension to the Babelsberg castle – estimated at 2.5 million marks – was stopped. The Lord Chamberlain postponed building indefinitely. It was only in 1911 that the plans were once again activated. The idea of expanding Schloss Babelsberg for this purpose had been thrown overboard. In the meantime, the successor had found his great-grandfather's neo-gothic castle too uncomfortable and its architecture no longer up to date. It is thought that a journey to England, made by the royal couple in 1911, provided the impulse to give the new castle the character of an English country house. On 6 May 1913 – his thirty-first birthday – the Crown Prince laid the foundation stone for his future residence. The Lord Chamberlain calculated that it would be completed in 1915. The architect Paul Schultze-Naumburg, who was experienced in building country houses,

The painting of Crown Prince William in the uniform of the Danzig Royal Hussars (1932) and the pastel of Crown Princess Cecilia (1934) are both works by the Berlin artist Bernhard Zickendraht (1854–1937).

Construction of Schloss Cecilienhof, summer 1914. With the exception of the main wing, the basic structure of the castle, begun in September 1913, was completed in April 1914. However, the outbreak of World War I slowed further building. In November 1917 – two years later than planned – Kaiser William II officially opened the castle.

was commissioned with planning and construction. Models were drafted in his famous atelier in Saaleck. The Crown Prince and Princess inspected the building site at irregular intervals. Various aspects of the building were determined by the royal couple, down to the tiniest detail. In this way, the conspicuous oriel front facing the lake was created at the express wish of the Prince. The couple's expenditure for holding court went far beyond that of the usual cost for a country house, forcing the architect to mislead them concerning the actual size by continuously regrouping and staggering the individual building elements. This resulted in several loosely connected sections grouped around a large courtyard as a driveway, a garden courtyard and three courtyards for service and housekeeping activities.

In August 1914, the basic structure of the house, constructed by the A. and F. Bolle Company from Potsdam, was completed and workers began covering the enormous roof. It was planned that work on the interior be completed in approximately one year. After the outbreak of war, the court building office ordered that work be ceased. Only a few craftsmen remained behind to safeguard the shell; the remaining bricklayers, carpenters and stonemasons all had to go to war. It soon became obvious that some shortcomings had appeared "due to a lack of proper supervision" – as the Lord Chamberlain Wolf Ferdinand von Stülpnagel recalled. Professor Schultze-Naumburg was a close friend of the Lord Chamberlain Count Bismarck-Bohlen and had generously turned a blind eye to some deficiencies in the construction. Seeing that there were no signs of the war coming to an end "and, because the country house without windows and doors was in danger of going to rack and ruin, the decision was made to continue with building". In 1915, construction was begun on the interior. Among others, Josef Wackerle was commissioned with the interior decoration. Work proceeded rapidly and the scaffolding was taken down in September 1916.

The prolonged war and the resulting shortages in manpower and construction materials led to a further year's delay in the completion of construc-

The former Crown Prince and Princess and their six children on the so-called 'photo steps' of Schloss Cecilienhof (1927). One year previously, in the 'prince's settlement', the Prussian state had decided that Cecilienhof remain in the possession of the state, but that the former Crown Prince and his family be granted rights of residence for three generations.

Menu for the silver wedding anniversary dinner of the Crown Prince and his wife in 1930. On 6 June, a private celebration, in the presence of William II, had already taken place in Doorn, in the Netherlands. Eight days later, on 14 June, William and Cecilia gave a dinner in Schloss Cecilienhof.

tion. The Crown Princess was not able to move in with her children until 14 August 1917. It was only at this time that the building received its name: Schloss Cecilienhof.

The Crown Prince hardly took any notice of the change in residence seeing that he was Commander-in-Chief of the 'Crown Prince's Battalion' on the western front. Three weeks after moving into Schloss Cecilienhof, the Crown Princess was delivered of her sixth child. The newly-born princess was christened Cecilia in the hall of Schloss Cecilienhof on 9 November 1917, in the presence of the Crown Prince and the Imperial couple. Exactly one year after the christening, on 9 November 1918, the November Revolution broke out, leading to the overthrow of the Hohenzollern throne. The Kaiser and Crown Prince fled into exile in the Netherlands and, after the revolution, the entire fortune of the House of Hohenzollern was confiscated and placed under the authority of the Prussian state. This was also the case with Schloss Cecilienhof, where the former Crown Princess continued to live until the end of 1920. The uncertainties concerning ownership and the lack of financial means forced her to give up the domicile in Potsdam. In order not to jeopardise their rights of residence, her two oldest sons, William and Louis Ferdinand, remained in the so-called Princes' Wing of Schloss Cecilienhof. Cecilia had decided to move to Oels, near Breslau, in Silesia with her four younger children. It was only after the 'princes' settlement' in 1926 that life once again returned to Cecilienhof. The settlement of the property dispute between the House of Hohenzollern and the Prussian state finally brought clarity into the status of the future rights of possession. Schloss Cecilienhof was to remain in the property of the state but the Crown Prince and his wife, their children and grandchildren were granted rights of residence. The Crown Prince, who was allowed to leave his exile in the Netherlands in 1923, moved back to Cecilienhof from Oels. He had always enjoyed Potsdam's proximity to the German capital of Berlin. Cecilia, on the other hand, preferred the Silesian renaissance castle as her residence and her sojourns in Potsdam were usually of a short duration. However, when they were in residence in Cecilienhof, it formed a rendezvous for the officers of the vanished monarchy, artists and intellectuals. The Crown Princess organised house concerts and, on most occasions, played piano herself. She invited famous artists, including the conductor Wilhelm Furtwängler, the pianists Elly Ney and Wilhelm Backhaus, the violinist Bronislaw Huberman, as well as the young Herbert von Karajan, to Cecilienhof. Since the 1930s, diplomats had, once again, started visiting the former Crown Prince's court. William Dodd, the ambassador of the USA, the French ambassador, André Francois-Poncet, and Josef Lipski, the Polish envoy, were often guests of the former royal couple.

Cecilia's nephew, Crown Prince Frederick of Denmark, made a private visit with his young wife to Potsdam. Frederick had married 25-year-old Swedish Princess Ingrid one year previously. William and Cecilia had taken part in the wedding in Copenhagen.

Close girlfriends of the Crown Princess, whom she had known since childhood, were always invited to lectures on art history and to evening entertainments. Schloss Oels, in the seclusion of Silesia, was the private refuge of the royal couple, whereas Schloss Cecilienhof took on the function of their official residence and place of representation for the family. It was here that the large family celebrations took place, such as the confirmation of the children in 1922, 1927 and 1934. The last great family reunion occurred in May 1938, when the second son of the Crown Prince married Grand Duchess Kira of Russia.

After the 1920s, the royal children left their parents' house, one by one, to continue their education in various cities. In 1936, only the Crown Prince and Princess and their youngest daughter, Cecilia, were permanent residents in Schloss Cecilienhof. After the beginning of World War II, the Crown Princess withdrew to her property in Silesia. The Crown Prince spent Christmas 1944 together with his wife in Cecilienhof. At the beginning of January 1945, Cecilia travelled once again to Oels for a few days. William left Schloss Cecilienhof on 17 January and moved to Oberstdorf, in Bavaria. During the last days of January 1945, when the Red Army had already conquered the city of Küstrin and it was feared that they could advance to Berlin in two days, Cecilia decided to leave Potsdam. Accompanied by her son Hubertus and his wife, she left Schloss Cecilienhof on 2 February 1945. As the last of the Hohenzollern family, Prince Oscar of Prussia – the Crown Prince's brother – lived in Cecilienhof after the departure of the other family members. When he was forced to leave the castle on 12 April 1945 the entire, precious furnishing was left behind.

The striking entrance portal of the castle is dominated by two chimneys, decorated with heraldic motives, and a large driveway which leads up to the inner courtyard.

Representation and Tradition –
The Apartments of the Crown Prince
and Princess in Changing Times

The Cour d'honneur: Priority for the Crown Prince

From afar, one can see the coats of arms on the two chimneys above the entrance portal, which bear witness to the original function of this house as the residence of the last German Crown Prince, William, and his wife, Cecilia. On one side, the skilfully-fired bricks are decorated with an eagle, the heraldic animal of the House of Hohenzollern and, on the other, an ox head as a symbol of the origin of the Crown Princess from the House of Mecklenburg-Schwerin. In the middle of the garden façade is the driveway for the approach of the Crown Prince and his wife and their noble guests. The opposite front of the house, facing the Jungfernsee (Maidens' Lake), with the striking, two-storey bay windows of the main hall, is the display side of the castle, intended to amaze the ship passengers sailing by. The former apartments of the Crown Prince and Princess, the guestrooms and dining rooms are grouped around the large cour d'honneur. In the centre of the courtyard, one's glance falls on a star of red plants which, as a symbol of the Potsdam Conference of 1945, is cultivated to this day and has permanently replaced the flower bed which used to grace the setting. The external appearance of the house is primarily characterised by the decorative half-timbering of the upper storey and through the combination of various materials, such as sandstone, wood and gravel finery adapted to harmonise with the existing landscape. Whereas most of the buildings show the typical characteristics of English country houses, some of the details, such as the semi-oval staircase tower in the south-eastern corner of the courtyard and the gatehouse, refer back to the building styles of medieval castles.

Immediately above the entrance gate, two shields with the coats of arms of the two dynasties and the date 1916 are a sign of the bond between William and Cecilia, bringing back memories of the first residents and the time the castle was built.

The covered driveway, in the form of a tripartite arcade with Tudor arches, cross vaults and wooden paving, was reserved for the Crown Prince and Princess and their noble guests and is still in use today as the main entrance to the castle rooms.

The eastern saddleback roof is crowned with a series of five chimneys fashioned on English models, whose conspicuous ornamentation demonstrates the importance of the private apartments and representation rooms of the royal couple, below. The large number of chimneys led to the castle being given the nickname 'chimneysweep academy'. However, not all the flues were in operation as fireplaces; some were connected to a sophisticated ventilation system.

The windows attract attention through their individually leaded panes: the corridors and rooms are located behind window panes with rectangular and lozenge-shaped patterns, whereas as the risalites and bay windows are accentuated by an extravagant diamond motive.

The elaborate chimney stacks appear to be red-brick sculptures and, in the interplay with the half-timbered gable, evoke the atmosphere of an English country house.

The Vestibule: The Entrée into the Last Hohenzollern Castle

Coming directly from the cour d'honneur, one enters a wooden-panelled, darkish room from where several doors open into the interior of the castle. A double door, opposite the entrance, leads into the great hall. This is bordered on the left and right by two galleries in front of the apartments of the Crown Prince and his wife.

The fireplace niche in the entrance hall was originally intended to be a cosy place in which to sit and its decoration reflects the taste of the time.

The vestibule is subdivided by pillars into two sections whose ceilings are emphasised by wooden rafters. The waxed-oak panelling reaches to door height and is divided into fields with a raised folded-linen pattern. The doors which are let into the panelling appear to be invisible and give only a hint of what lies beyond them. A large, wooden-framed fireplace recess, vaulted with a Tudor arch, dominates the right side of the north wall and gives the room a cosy atmosphere with its wood carving and carefully laid bricks.

The oak panelling, with its classic folded-linen pattern fusing art and craftsmanship, seems modest and, at the same time, noble. The décor, inspired by England, gives the room an unmistakable character that is unique in Germany.

The Main Hall and the Conference Room: Tudor Romanticism with a Round Table

The Main Hall, twelve metres high and rising over two storeys, is vaulted with an apparently wooden-beam ceiling which looks like the upturned hull of a ship and which can be understood as an allusion to the Crown Princess's passion for seafaring. The beams appear to be massive but are merely disguised with boards and only simulate genuine timbers. The decorative half-timbering of the gable, which seems worthy of an English country seat, is also only an imitation and has more a decorative than structural function. Here, the beams are also embellished with the coats of arms of the two dynasties: the ox head of the Mecklenburgs over the window and the Prussian eagle above the staircase. The bay window which soars over the two storeys has ninety-eight leaded panes in a colossal outward-jutting sandstone frame.

The walls are panelled to two-thirds in oak and are subdivided into simple rectangles, giving the room a certain feeling of comfort, despite its size. The double doors, with their elaborately profiled panelling, mark the entrance to the royal apartments, where, traditionally, the lord and lady had separate living quarters. Both the passage and the enormous fireplace recess are spanned by Tudor arches. The magnificent fireplace, with its massive sandstone surround, decorated with martial motives, forms an indispensable part of an English country house. The former musicians' gallery is hidden behind four openings between the boiserie and ceiling. Even though the planned organ was never installed, it was possible to provide music for the family festivities from there.

The visual focus of the room is provided by the monumental staircase, which not only provides a connection to the private apartments on the upper floor but also draws the attention of visitors. It was carved out of oak and presented to the Crown Prince and his wife by the city parliament of Danzig in honour of his sojourn in the metropolis on the Baltic Sea. As Commander of

This historic photograph shows the hearth in the hall during the era of the Crown Prince. The tiger skin is probably a trophy from 1910, when William took part in an "expedition through the fairy-tale land of India", as the Crown Princess later wrote.

The staircase, with its neo-baroque form, somewhat breaks the uniformity of the English-dominated hall, but harmonises with the overall feeling of the room. Here, the architect was able to integrate both styles in an eloquent fashion. Sturdy, flowing acanthus vines flank, as stringers, the stairs and elaborate carving decorates the banisters and balustrades.

The Living Hall is the largest room and the heart of the castle. Until 1945, it was the scene of many family events. The main staircase leads to the private apartments of the Crown Prince and Princess on the upper floor.

the 1st Royal Hussar Regiment, William was assigned to Danzig-Langfuhr from 1911 to 1913. During his stationing there, he was made an honorary member of the Woodturners Guild, which received the commission for the magnificent staircase for Schloss Cecilienhof. William had learned the craft of woodturning during his training at the Plönen cadet school in Schleswig-Holstein.

As a result of the austerities caused by the war, the original furnishing of the Main Hall consisted of a series of pieces collected from various warehouses and other castles and appears somewhat improvised. The combination of exquisite old pieces and undistinguished modern furniture can also be interpreted as a conscious profession to a form of English cosiness, which was regarded as exemplary. Unfortunately, during the preparations for the Potsdam Conference, many pieces of furniture from the Crown Prince's apartments were removed to the nearby dairy and probably destroyed in the fire of 18 July 1945. Only the lanterns survived this period. Today, the furnishings are dedicated to the Potsdam Conference and show the condition in 1945: the

In 1945, the Living Hall was converted into the conference hall for the Potsdam Conference, with the huge, round table offering place for the 15 representatives of the American, British and Soviet delegations. The armchairs were reserved for the heads of state, the other chairs were used by the foreign ministers and their deputies, the ambassadors and interpreters. The chairs which today stand against the wall were for the military and political advisers, and the minute-takers sat at the six desks which were placed in the centre of the room during the conference.

large round table, with a diameter of 3.05 m, was probably produced in a furniture factory in Moscow and set up in the main hall especially for the conference. The chairs were part of the furnishings of the Niederländische Palais (Netherlands Palace) in Berlin, where the general administration of the, previously reigning, Prussian royal family was located before World War II.

The leaders of the victorious Allies of World War II entered the plenary hall through the double doors on the side, having prepared themselves for the meetings in the apartments of the Crown Prince and his wife which had been converted into offices. The middle door was opened only briefly to enable the accredited photoreporters to take pictures of the conference activities. Even today, the visitor can sense the aura of this exceptional location, where, in the summer of 1945, momentous decisions were taken which would influence global politics.

A glimpse at the 'bargaining table' during the consultations of the 'Big Three'. The photo was taken on 28 July 1945, after Atlee, the new British Prime Minister, had replaced Churchill and continued negotiations with American President Truman and the Soviet leader, Stalin.

The Princess's Music Salon: Reminiscences of the Marble Palace

This long room, which is also called the White Salon, was intended to remind Cecilia of the happy days she had spent in the Marble Palace. One can identify many details of its concert hall in the White Salon. Bearers, supported by two Corinthian pillars, transverse the room, dividing it into three sections. The central section, which is heightened by a vault, achieves its charm through the relief-like plaster medallions with allegories of the four seasons and the filigree floral wreath around the ceiling. The large central rosette of the parquet floor, made out of oak, maple and cedar wood, also relates to Frederick William II's concert hall in the Marble Palace. The warm hues of the wood of the floor correspond with the monochrome white of the walls and ceiling and give the room the appearance of a harmonious ensemble.

The instruments and flowers in the supraports above the doors awaken the spirit of the room: harps, flutes and fanfares are accompanied by drums, trumpets and a tambourine. Violins, a lute and even a bagpipe complete the

Five large French windows open onto the wide terrace, allowing light to flood into the room, where it is reflected by the white of the walls and ceiling. The carvings in the recesses, made by Josef Wackerle (1880–1959), represent mythological scenes and hide bare heating pipes.

musical intermezzo. The plaster reliefs were created by Josef Wackerle, who was also responsible for the skilfully carved coverings of the heating in the window niches. The grotesques, with their depiction of antique gods, perfectly disguise the mundane use. In each of the five window axes, Fortuna, Juno, Apollo, Diana and Hebe stand as pendants to each other.

The seemingly classicistic fireplace is flanked by two busts of King Friedrich William II and Queen Luisa, which were modelled in 1812 by Christian Philipp Wolff. The chalices on both sides of the mantelpiece clock came from the Crown Prince's Palace in Berlin and their inscriptions show that they commemorate the marriage of William and Cecilia on 6 June 1905. The watercolour was painted by Angelos Giallina, an artist from Corfu. Empress Elisabeth of Austria (Sisi) was also very fond of his landscapes and commissioned several of them for the Achilleion on the Ionian island, which the Austrian court consequently sold to Kaiser William II.

The two floor vases and flower pots in front of the fireplace were produced at the beginning of the twentieth century by the porcelain factory in St Petersburg and presented to the bride and groom for their wedding. They are an indication of the family connections between the Crown Princess and the House of Romanov. The chandelier was also a part of the original decor-

Imperial porcelain and faience, as well as painted glassware, are displayed in the showcases. The wafer-thin blue carafes and candy bowls, champagne, wine and liqueur glasses made of Venetian glass from the island of Murano and decorated with Bacchic dancers, were a gift from the Italian King Victor Emanuel III to the Crown Prince and his wife.

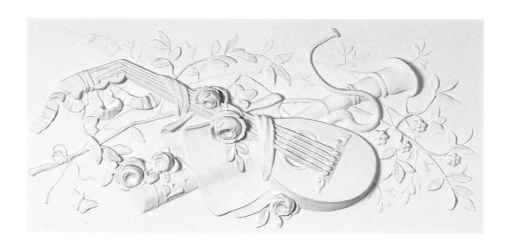

Floral and musical elements are harmoniously united in the reliefs above the doors. Here, blossoms, twigs and garlands swirl around a lute, sheets of music and a bassoon.

The Crown Princess's music salon is the most interesting room in the castle, from the point of view of art history. It was completely remodelled for the Potsdam Conference and only the decoration of the fireplace reminds one of former times. It is said that at the beginning of negotiations in 1945, Stalin played host to the other participants at a reception given in this room.

ation of the room and is one of the few remaining original lighting fixtures in the castle.

The salon, which was previously furnished in Louis Seize style and had a grand piano, was one of the favourite rooms of the Crown Prince and his wife and was used to receive high-level guests and for house concerts.

Today, the interior of the room gives the impression of being part of the Soviet sphere of influence at the time of the Potsdam Conference. The classicistic furniture gives the false impression of the former appearance of the room but, as a feature of the conference equipment, should not be replaced.

Each delegation to the conference demanded an individual entrance and separate offices. For Joseph Stalin, the Soviet Premier and Communist Party leader, the French window on the right-hand side was opened and the adjacent room, which can be entered through a narrow glass door, furnished.

The Crown Princess's Writing Room and the Soviet Office: A Salon for a Lady and a Dictator

It was possible to reconstruct the original red, silk damask wallcovering with its vine pattern, which was replaced by a rose-coloured wallpaper made of synthetic fibre during renovations carried out in the 1930s. One specific architectural feature is the hexagonal bay window with leaded glass panes, whose diamond shape emphasise the hierarchy of the rooms of the house. At the fireplace, accentuated by blue, eighteenth-century Dutch tiles, the viewer's attention is drawn to the painting hanging above it – a view of the Villa Falconieri near Rome painted by Alfred Hertel in 1911. Hertel was one of the first to receive a grant from Kaiser William II, who had purchased the villa to sponsor young artists, and it was there that Hertel established his outstanding reputation as a landscape painter. To the right of the fireplace, a hidden door leads to the neighbouring writing room of the Crown Princess.

The built-in bookcases still store a part of the Crown Prince's library, which was moved from its location in the Marble Palace in 1917 and managed to survive the turmoil of history. The bookcases, like the panelling, doors and window surroundings, are made of varnished mahogany and were not made lockable until the castle was

Cecilia's passion for collecting is obvious in the writing room. A model ship and the chandelier topped with a frigate make one immediately aware of the Crown Princess's love of seafaring.

During the Potsdam Conference, the room called the Red Salon was decorated functionally and soberly, in keeping with Stalin's taste. Only the fireplace and bookcases are still in the original state.

transformed into a museum after 1952. The French books and a volume of Russian poetry on the shelves bear witness to the Crown Princess's multi-lingual talents, which were no doubt aided by her lengthy sojourns on the Côte d'Azur and frequent visits to her grandfather near St Petersburg.

The furnishing consisted of a hotchpotch of chairs, tables and cabinets, which were decorated with flowers, photographs and numerous knick-knacks, making the room seem rather cluttered.

The events of 1945 have also left their traces on this room. A living-room suite of smooth leather now takes pride of place in the oriel, and in the middle of the room stand the obligatory desk and chairs of the generalissimo. The massive, unadorned mahogany desk gained a rather unsuitable addition with the dynamically carved armchair. The support services of the Soviet army, who were responsible for the preparations for the conference, simply trans-ported furniture from the other Potsdam castles and the villas in Babelsberg and near the Neuer Garten into the designated conference rooms. What remains is the magnificent view into the Prince's garden, where the Crown Princess could watch her children at play and – in the distance – of the water of the Holy Lake shimmering among the majestic trees.

The two facets of the history of the castle come together in the alcove of the Soviet office: the original lead-paned windows allow light to flow over the massive leather furniture of the conference era.

The Ship's Cabin: A Passion for Navigation

Cecilia's weakness for navigation played a major role in the decoration of her private apartments. Along with her husband, she undertook extensive cruises. The Crown Princess followed the economic boom in the shipbuilding industry in Germany with great interest. On 1 December 1906, and as the name giver, she christened an intercontinental steamship of the North German Lloyd Company 'Crown Princess Cecilia'. Built at the Vulkan shipyard in Stettin, it was one of the most modern ships of its day. On 29 March 1914, shortly after construction of the Cecilienhof began, she inspected the passenger steamship 'Columbus' on the occasion of its christening at the Schichau shipyard in Danzig and was exceptionally enthusiastic about its stylish interior decoration. The luxury liner, built on the commission of the North German Lloyd Company, was regarded as being absolutely unique – both technically and artistically – and had to be handed over to Great Britain after World War I as part of Germany's reparations. To a great extent, the designs for the cabin decoration stem from Paul Ludwig Troost, whose fame as an interior decorator and furniture designer was greater than his reputation as Germany's leading ship architect. Later, he designed some of the most important Nazi buildings, including the Haus der Deutschen Kunst (House of German Art) in Munich. It is probable that Cecilia's esteem of Troost's talent led to his being commissioned with planning the decoration of her private apartments in Schloss Cecilienhof, where construction had recently commenced. This small room, designed like a cabin, is part of the suite which leads from the representational rooms on the ground floor to the private quarters on the first. The Crown Princess could reach her bedroom and dressing room over a small staircase.

With the exception of a novel sliding window in the form of a porthole, which, supposedly, sailors had brought to the building site from a decommissioned yacht, the decoration is based on Troost's plans. Both the ceiling and walls, as well as the furniture, are made of white-painted pinewood. The blue, printed-linen curtains and upholstery, along with the lamps and other accessories perfect the maritime atmosphere. Cecilia attended to her morning correspondence seated at the desk and took elevenses on the comfortable sofa. The firmly-anchored cupboards and commodes, as well as the tiny washing niche disguised as a cabinet, are just as typical of a ship as the water flanges on the doors. The imitation of a slanted mast increases the illusion of a real cabin, in which such a construction would hardly be imaginable. There is, however, no motor to simulate the movements of a ship – even though a legend to this effect existed for many years.

The ship's cabin is not only unique on account of its unusual décor, but also because it is the only room in the castle preserved in its original condition.

The washbasin *en miniature* disappears almost completely in a cupboard and was intended more as a prop in the cabin than for practicality.

The Crown Princess was able to work undisturbed at this delicate desk with its view over the Prince's Garden and still feel as if she were on a sailing yacht. The clock with the porcelain face is an allusion to Cecilia's love of roses.

The Crown Prince's Smoking Salon and the American Office: Tasteful Elegance for a Chain-Smoker and a President

The difference between the mostly bright and cheerful rooms of the lady of the house on the one side and the darkly-panelled gentleman's rooms on the other is immediately apparent. The Crown Prince, a heavy smoker, was given a salon planned in keeping with his demands and with a pinewood coffered ceiling designed to catch the smoke. William justified his passion with the English way of life and, on social occasions, only grudgingly abstained from smoking

The doors, which are integrated into the panelling, and the bookcases, set into the walls and containing an additional portion of the Crown Prince's library, lend the room a feeling of harmony. Even the impressive fireplace, with its mantel of oak and sandstone, blends perfectly with the structure of the room. The salon had comparatively spartan furnishings, with various places to sit and smokers' tables. The furnishings were removed and replaced with pieces from the Marble Palace to create the office of the American President. One can only wonder whether the catastrophic atomic bombings of Hiroshima and Nagasaki on 6 and 9 August 1945 were the subject of discussion in this room between Truman and his advisers. In any case, the disaster of hundreds of thousands of Japanese took its inexorable course in Potsdam after Japan rejected the demands of the USA, Great Britain and China for its unconditional surrender. By way of sanction, the three major powers threatened

The Crown Prince became an advertising personality for the brand of cigarettes which bore his name and showed him in his Royal Hussar's uniform, framed by the Prussian eagle and crowns. The cigarettes were produced by the 'Egyptian Cigarette Company' of Ludwig Przedecki, the 'Court Cigarette Manufacturer of his Imperial and Royal Highness the Crown Prince of the German Empire and of Prussia', and cost eight pfennigs each. The unique feature of the cigarette was the patented straw mouthpiece and William's monogram beneath a crown.

The living and smoking room of the Crown Prince was originally decorated very functionally. This historic photograph shows a suite which still exists and which, today, is exhibited in the former bedroom of the Crown Prince and Princess.

Today, the Crown Prince's salon is distinguished only by its furnishings flush with the walls. The classicistic mahogany furniture with the tasteful desk do not blend in with the otherwise English surroundings. They were a reference to President Truman.

the Japanese people with absolute annihilation in the Potsdam Declaration of 26 July 1945. After the successful atomic bomb test in the New Mexico desert on 16 July 1945, Truman was set on ending the war in the Far East through the employment of a new weapon of unimaginable explosive force. On 24 July 1945, Truman offhandedly informed Stalin of the change in the world's balance of power, which was now in the USA's favour. As a result, work on an atomic bomb was intensified – and the nuclear arms race took its course.

The Crown Prince's Library and the British Office: Books and Hunting Scenes for a Passionate Huntsman and a Prime Minister

Approximately 2,000 volumes from the collection of the Crown Prince and Princess were stored in the (originally open) built-in bookcases. The inventory shows a cross-section of almost all literary genres: valuable encyclopaedias and the multi-volume lexicons of Meyer and Brockhaus stood alongside works on German and international history. A great deal of space was devoted to historical and military treatises. In addition to biographies of the Hohenzollern family, they contained precise descriptions of Prussian regiments, lists of ranks and decorations, as well as political, scientific and cultural publications. Even the memoirs of William and Cecilia are included. A large number of English-language editions is proof of the Crown Prince's close ties to the British Empire. His journeys through Great Britain and his predilection for English clothing and the lifestyle of the country led to what was, at the time, the dubious reputation of being anglophile. They did, however, help him to a considerable knowledge of the language so that these books cannot merely be regarded as a façade. Fiction, travel literature by Baedecker and rare bibliophile publications, including a noble edition of Brehm's *Animal Lives* with gold embossing on the spine, round off the picture. The 'collected correspondence', almanacs, state and court calendars, and genealogical notebooks were no less important as significant elements of the library. Bookplates created by famous artists can be found inside many of the books which belonged to William and Cecilia, as well to Kaiser William II and Empress Augusta Victoria.

The plaster frieze, running round the room and depicting native and exotic wild animals, is an indication of the Crown Prince's passion for hunting. He maintained the hunting tradition of the house and, just like the Kaiser, enjoyed stag hunting on Rominten Heath in East Prussia. The scenery is dominated not only by red deer; one can also see a wild boar, a dog and two wood grouse. Opposite, an elephant, a chamois and a lion bring back

The proof of ownership in many volumes is evidence that they belonged to the Crown Prince's library. In this *ex libris*, created for Cecilia in 1906, the court engraver G. Otto based his design on one of William's bookplates from 1903.

William and Cecilia often immortalised themselves through entries in their books, in their own handwriting. The Crown Prince signed his memoirs, published in 1922, on his 40th birthday on 6 May. The Crown Princess gave her youngest son, Frederick, a novel with the dedication, "To Fritzi from Mama, Christmas 1930".

It was possible to relax around the fireplace, reading one of the many books which have managed to survive the historic changes almost unscathed. The Delft tiles on the fireplace wall, however, were removed after the war and replaced by white ones.

The conference decoration, with neo-gothic furniture from Schloss Babelsberg, appears somewhat out of place in the library. It was meant to give Prime Minister Churchill a feeling of home.

The value of the former library is due not only to its large number of books but also to its filigree ceiling decoration. Josef Wackerle was probably inspired by an illustration of a magnificent ceiling in a volume on English country houses when executing the stucco work.

reminiscences of the Crown Prince's hunting experiences in Ceylon and India.

Thematically, these animal portrayals create a link to the former hunting room lying above and reachable over a secret stairway. This room, with its large bay window, probably served the Crown Prince as an additional study. Alongside a view of Constantinople, painted by Ernst Körner in 1873, there is a painting of the Kaiser William Memorial Church in Berlin. This was painted by Ulrich in 1943 and shows the intact building, erected between 1891 and 1895 by Franz Schwechten in the late romantic style of the Rhineland. After World War II, its ruins became a symbol of West Berlin.

In 1945, the room was furnished for the British prime minister with neo-gothic objects from Babelsberg Castle. The maple desk was previously in the bedroom of Kaiser William I. The octagonal table, with its spirally twisted central column, set in the bay window and the four upholstered chairs were formerly in the Kaiser's workroom. On the other hand, the origin of the blue velvet suite with the enormous clawed feet on the other side of the room is still unsolved.

The Breakfast Room: A Breath of Sanssouci

Compared with the other rooms, nowhere is the atmosphere so fundamentally different than in the octagonal breakfast room, which served as a transition between the living quarters and dining room. It is crowned with a polygonal dome and its restrained rococo-like illumination creates the impression of a garden pavilion. Cheerful grisaille painting over the doors and windows symbolise the four seasons: one putto with a small basket and butterfly appears as a harbinger of spring; another, with sunhat, sickle and bundle of corn, heralds the summer; the next one ushers in autumn with his rattle and a hare; and, finally, a small skater with a fur collar, muff and cap is the embodiment of winter. Josef Wackerle produced a masterpiece of carving with his three-door covering for the heating. The ornate pinewood reliefs represent scenes from everyday life, along with carved floral bouquets full of variation. The ornament on the left makes allusions to the corn harvest with its basket, ears of corn, hat and scythe; the central one illustrates the wine harvest with its jugs, grapes, and panpipes as well as a shepherd's crook and Bacchic staff; and, on the right, we see an allegory of fishing with a creel, net, paddle and trident.

A further historic photograph taken by Marta Huth shows the Breakfast Room in 1925. The naturalistic décor of the walls contrasts with the dark oak panelling in the adjoining rooms and gives the room a special style – unlike an English country house.

The 'Ceres Service', with its sculptural decoration of golden ears of wheat and fantastic fruit and blossoms, is completely in the style of Jugendstil, which the Crown Princess greatly admired. The brilliant coloration of the décor on a white ground also creates a stylistic bridge to the Biedermeier period. Tiny baskets of flowers serve as knobs, cornucopias form handles and the plates and dishes are decorated with perforated borders.

The carved coverings of the heating – with their subtle handling of the wood and the richness of the floral garlands, graphic motives, ribbons and delicate ornamentation – are regarded as a gem of craftsmanship.

Even today, the Breakfast Room has lost little of its charm. The illusionist painting, with the colourful arrangements of fruits and flowers as well as pheasants and wood grouse, gives the room a sense of lightness and freshness and the feeling of a bower. In the showcases, the few pieces of the Ceres Service which have been preserved give a first-rate impression of the former magnificence of the ensemble. The centrepiece and oyster dishes are exemplary of this artistic refinement.

The charm of the original ceiling lamp receives its full value through the floral elements of pale green Venetian glass and crystal. The floral lampshades and fronds bowed like feathers once again reflect the bower-like atmosphere of the room.

The furnishing only hints at the original condition and can be dated around the time of the construction of the castle.

The so-called 'Ceres Service', named after the goddess of fertility, was designed by Theo Schmuz-Baudiss, who had been the artistic director of the KPM since 1908. Here, we are dealing with pieces from the jubilee service commissioned in 1913 to celebrate the 150th anniversary of Königliche Porzellan-Manufaktur Berlin (Royal Porcelain Factory), which was founded by Frederick the Great in 1763. Using simple forms, in the classical style, Schmuz-Baudiss created a successful synthesis between tradition and modernity.

The Guest Apartments: Royal Visitors
to the Crown Prince and Princess

If members of the family or of other European royal houses visited the Crown Prince and his wife, they had to be accommodated in an appropriate fashion. A guest apartment with a living room, bedroom and dressing room, as well as baths and servants' quarters, was available for Cecilia's Mecklenburg relations. It was located directly next to the royal rooms on the ground floor of the main building and led to the section being called the 'Mecklenburg Wing'.

The living room, with its plain half-timbering and beamed ceiling could be reached both from the corridor as well as from the Prince's Garden. In the adjoining bedroom one can still see the alcove for the bed and in the dressing room next to this, a built-in wardrobe. This suite of rooms was used by the Soviet Foreign Minister Molotov and his deputy Wyschinski as their offices during the Potsdam Conference in 1945.

The more elegant suite was on the upper storey above the entrance and was reserved for princely guests. The view towards the main courtyard allowed prominent guests to live in the standard to which they were accustomed. The guest book lists names such as Queen Victoria Eugenia of Spain and Queen Alexandrina of Denmark. The Crown Princess's elder sister had married the Danish Crown Prince and later King Christian X and, during her visits, took up lodgings on the *bel étage*.

The ensemble consisted of a living room and bedroom as well as a bath and servant's

Unfortunately, the appearance of the guest apartment in the 'Mecklenburg Wing' has changed completely. Two historic photographs give an impression of the decoration from the era of the Crown Prince: one room functioned as a simply decorated lounge with a fireplace and a separate exit to the garden through the open door on the right; the second photo shows the spacious closet in the dressing room, where the playful decoration of the wallpaper is repeated in the chair covering.

room. The living room was decorated with a green-striped silk wallcovering and the ceiling with stucco. The adjacent bedroom was panelled in elegant pinewood, bordered in white. The bed alcove was given a covering of cloth printed with roses and doves. The furniture, placed against the walls, consisted of a three-door wardrobe and a dressing table with mirror and gilded relief carving, in a light, matt-lacquer finish, giving the room both neo-classicistic and Biedermeier accents.

Several pieces from the original furnishings can be seen in the comfortable guest apartment above the castle entrance. Among these are the marble-topped console table and mirror in the bedroom.

Princely Dining and Lodgings – The Historical Rooms in the Castle Hotel

The Dining Room and Terrace: A Feast for the Senses

The dining room, which followed on from the living rooms, was, along with the main hall, the social centre of the house. The dark oaken panelling which covered the entire walls underlined the special importance of this room within the castle and, in addition to the desired cosiness, created the appropriate dignity for a noble banquet. In his decoration for the elaborately worked cassettes of the panelling, the architect Schultze-Naumburg once again adopted English models from the relevant literature. Where Schultze-Naumburg more or less copied the rhombic-formed coffer forms, Wackerle made use only of basic elements of the English country-house style for the door frames and fillings, adapting them in accordance with his own expertise. The large opening of the fireplace is lined with bricks arranged to great effect and vaulted with a lightly curved Tudor arch. Pilasters on both sides of the sandstone mantel seem to support the massive upper part of the fireplace, which is subdivided into three relief areas. The middle section is dominated by the two coats of arms of the royal couple – the ox head and eagle – and flanked by two realistic

Unlike today, the table was formerly set only for the Crown Prince's family and their guests. At larger gatherings, the tables were moved closer together and decorated festively – just as in the Castle Restaurant today. As the boiserie, fireplace and stucco ceiling have been preserved, the room has managed to retain much of its unique charm up to the present time.

The plaster relief of a cog on a stormy sea, with the Prussian eagle emblazoned on its sail, on the ceiling of the Dining Room takes its place thematically in the canon of maritime romanticism of the castle.

The wood fireplace surround, oriented on classic renaissance forms, bears Wackerle's hand and the carver's technical prowess makes it one of the showpieces of the castle.

The extravagant carving above the fireplace connects the importance of the Dining Room with the Crown Prince and his wife's memories of places which played an important role in their lives: the silhouette of the city of Danzig, synonym for the carefree years before World War I, and Oels Castle, the refuge and second home after the end of the monarchy. Between the scenes, the caryatides with baskets of fruit and wine chalices are an expression of pleasure and cheerfulness, as is the potpourri of various fruits and vines on the massive moulding.

landscapes: on the left, Schloss Oels in Silesia and, on the right, the old city of Danzig, with its typical gabled houses and, towering above, the famous Mary Church, built in the 14th and 15th centuries.

Two secret doors, hidden in the panelling, lead us into the adjoining breakfast room and, opposite, into the former serving room. This was the start of the service wing, where, in addition to the kitchen, the china and silver chambers – including a safe for the silver and a room for cleaning it – were located. A storage room for linens, an ironing room and laundry were also there, as were the pantries and a place for washing dishes. The former dining room for the household staff adjoined the rooms where food was prepared and was kept consciously different from the area of the nobility. Four double-winged French windows opened onto a large terrace which, because of its location, was lit up by the evening sun. A loggia made it possible to dine outside in a small group, even when it was raining. A sunken lawn was framed by colourful flowerbeds. The surrounding path and the open flight of steps invited one to take an after-dinner stroll, particularly in spring, when the magnolia was in full bloom and one's eye was enchanted by the beauty of the park. Today, this magnificent environment also houses the Castle Restaurant – which has an excellent reputation for its first-rate cuisine going far beyond the borders of Potsdam and Berlin and which can be recommended as a top gastronomic location.

During warm weather, the terrace of the Dining Room, crowned with the magnificent view over the adjacent garden parterre and the picturesque park landscape, invites one to dine outdoors.

The Marshal's Table: Gentlemen around the Fireplace

The Marshal's Table Room then and now: the room, which was once the private domain of the Crown Prince, is now open to hotel guests for festive receptions and conferences. The typical English character has remained even though the interior has been adapted to meet modern requirements.

In contrast to the dining room, the Marshal's Table, which can be reached over a separate staircase, was reserved for small parties in intimate surroundings. The Crown Prince liked to entertain his gentlemen friends in this almost medieval atmosphere, in which he could indulge in memories with Army officers and give free rein to his Berlin dialect. The gentlemen sat together around small tables while a crackling fire burned in the open hearth. Cecilia very rarely took part in these social events and, after dinner, retired to her apartments as quickly as possible.

Here, the beamed-ceiling construction also follows English models and, with its lowered crossbeams, appears to be just as overwhelming as the main hall. The wooden panelling, the covering of the heating, and the crest of the fireplace are made of darkly stained pinewood but are kept simpler than in the dining room beneath and accentuate the rustic atmosphere of this room. Today, the Marshal's Table Room is one of the castle hotel's most popular venues for banquets and conferences and provides space for up to eighty people.

The Personnel Quarters – 'Nuns' in the Service of the Crown Prince

If one goes back downstairs from the Marshal's Table Room, a corridor on the court side opens into a generous lobby leading to a wide staircase and several small rooms, which were formerly used for the telephone switchboard and other offices. The rooms for the staff were on the upper storey and were organised to meet the demands of a modern court. The narrow corridor leading towards the Marshal's Table was jokingly called the 'nuns' corridor' because it was here that the quarters of the unmarried female domestic staff was located. The strict separation of the sexes was as much a characteristic of a Victorian sense of morality as was the protection of privacy. Mutual respect and trust played a major role when living under one roof.

Obtaining a position in the royal household was extremely sought after, for it brought with it many privileges and social protection. Reliability, honesty and loyalty were prerequisites for being employed. A multitude of benefits – including free food and board, clothing, above-average pay and presents at Christmas time and for service anniversaries – were given in return for unconditional loyalty towards the family, being permanently on hand, and absolute discretion. The Crown Prince made a point of seeing that his staff members were suitably taken care of and often informed himself of their satisfaction. This not only made him well liked but also assured him that in politically difficult times he could rely on those in his employ.

The gracious staircase in the west wing leads directly from the central living area to the Marshal's Table Room – a masterpiece in which functionality and aesthetics are united in perfect harmony.

The Princes' Wing and the Princes' Courtyard – Rooms with a View

There was a separate entrance to the castle for the children of the Crown Prince and Princess which, with its carving and the bay window above it, appears more restrained than the two main portals. At the end of a small lobby, one passes through a compact oak door under a Tudor arch and enters a spacious hall whose furnishing as a lounge with a fireplace makes it seem quite cosy. Corridors lead off in two directions and, between them, a magnificent staircase leads up to the apartments of William and Cecilia's children and their servants. The rooms of the chamberlain and governor were located on the one side and the rooms of the ladies-in-waiting on the other. The chamberlain supervised the lives of the princes and princesses and was required to be able

The foyer of the Princes' Wing fulfilled the function of linking all the rooms necessary for the organisation of the everyday life of the children and facilitated orientation in this narrow and winding section of the house.

to inform the parents of their whereabouts at any time. The governor was responsible for the security of the house and its residents. The museum shop is now located in his former apartment, between the prince's entrance and main portal.

The spacious corridors on the upper floor were used mainly for the accommodation and tutelage of the princes and princesses. In addition to individual living rooms, bedrooms and bathrooms, the children also had their own dining room, a tea kitchen and a schoolroom. The rooms of the tutors were located only a short distance away and create a transition to the gate wing, where the living and working quarters of the senior staff members were situated.

The longstanding adjutant and personal advisor, Louis Müldner von Mülnheim, who worked for the Crown Prince after 1916, remained loyal in the last days of the war and stayed behind in Cecilienhof to protect the castle from plundering. He committed suicide in his rooms on 26 April 1945, when the Red Army entered Potsdam, and was buried in an unmarked grave in the New Garden, near the castle.

The Crown Princess's ladies-in-waiting were given small apartments with a living room and bedroom, bath and maid's chamber. During their transformation into hotel rooms, their appearance was fundamentally altered, taking the aspects of monument preservation and architecture into consideration.

The present-day form of the Prince's Garden is based on a later version. Originally, this section of the garden was hardly planted. Today, with its luxuriant flower beds and abundance of blooms and colours, it has become a pleasure ground, where the artistically pruned yews stimulate the fantasies of its visitors.

The close connection between the offspring's tract and the rooms of the lady of the house conformed to the principles of a Victorian household and led to the children being permanently under supervision. Her motherly care covered all areas of everyday life, including the children's education, whereas the Crown Prince and his sons had a more or less comradely relationship.

A three-arched arcade forms the lower storey of the north wing next to the Prince's Garden. This divides the romantic courtyard, whose middle point, since 1976, has been a small fountain surrounded by colourful flower beds.

A door beneath an arcade leads into the princes' playroom with its noteworthy fireplace. This room once provided an entrance into the park through its previously open vestibule. The gable above this is one of the most attractive half-timber constructions of the castle. In the adjoining Prince's Garden, colourful summer flowers, bushes and precisely lined-up succulents are united to form a unique botanical concert. This is most conspicuous with the artistically pruned small yews, whose appearance stimulates the visitor's fantasy. Benches invite one to linger, to take in the charm of the convoluted construction once again. The numerous gables and bay windows, as well as the various patterns and materials of the half-timber sections attract one's attention. The four richly decorated chimneys, compressed to a single complex, and, above all, the large bay window of the bedroom at the north-eastern

corner of the house make an indelible impression on the stroller. The architecturally remarkable ensemble is complemented by the wide terrace in front of the White Salon.

In 1960, the East German state travel agency opened the Schlosshotel (Castle Hotel) in the Cecilienhof as a hotel for the privileged few; in 1989, private operators took over. Today, the staff of the Relexa Hotel Group take care of the well-being of their guests, who are accommodated in rooms in keeping with the style of the house and who enjoy the first-rate service offered.

The basin of the fountain, with the bronze Narcissus seated on it, formerly stood in the Rose Garden of the New Palace in the park of Sanssouci. It was created by Hubert Netzer in 1896 and portrays the young man enamoured of his own reflection, with his attributes – shepherd's crook and goatskin – lying on the outer rim of the fountain.

The gable above the entrance to the Princes' Playroom, where only the brick fireplace is really noteworthy and the entrance was previously open, is counted among the most attractive half-timbered constructions of the castle and captivates one with the richness of its decorative forms.

Crown Princess Cecilia of Prussia

Cecilia, the youngest daughter of Grand Duke Friedrich Franz III of Mecklenburg and his wife, Russian Grand Duchess Anastasia Michailovna, was born on 20 September 1886 in Schwerin Castle. She received a strict education but, in the house of Mecklenburg, great emphasis was placed on multifaceted schooling. Cecilia had a command of several foreign languages, including English and Russian. It was during the wedding celebrations for her brother Friedrich Franz IV that the young duchess met her future husband. William was immediately overwhelmed by her beauty, her jet-black hair, the impressive eyes and her slim figure. On 5 September 1904, Cecilia and William celebrated their engagement at the Gelbensande hunting castle near Rostock.

The marriage festivities in Berlin, which lasted for four days, began on 3 June 1905 with the entrance of the young bride. The festive days were filled with con-certs, church services, receptions and visits to the Royal Opera House. The magnificent climax was the church wedding on the evening of 6 June in the chapel of the Royal Castle. Six children were born up until 1917. After the marriage, Cecilia found herself a member of one of the most powerful European dynasties. In the Prussian order of precedence she, as Crown Princess, followed immediately after the imperial couple and her husband. She bore the official title of 'Crown Princess of the German Empire and of Prussia' and, as the wife of the successor, was addressed as 'Imperial Highness'. Cecilia was one of the most elegant ladies of the imperial age and became a fashion ideal.

At first, the Crown Prince and his wife had the Marble Palace on the Holy Lake in Potsdam at their disposal as a summer residence. In the winter months, they lived in the impressive Crown Prince's Palace on Berlin's magnificent Unter den Linden boulevard. After 1917, the family lived in the newly-constructed Schloss Cecilienhof, where her daily life followed a fixed course. "Our family life takes up almost all my time and energy", she wrote in her memoirs. Cecilia – along with her hus-band – was excluded from daily political activities, for Kaiser William II would tolerate no interference in his authoritarian style of governing. Her main duty, there-fore, consisted of representing the imperial house as its leading female personality.

With the outbreak of World War I, Cecilia was given additional responsibilities and she devoted herself to substantial charity work. The Empress entrusted the Crown Princess with the welfare of the wounded soldiers in the military hospitals in Berlin and West Prussia. On Cecilia's initiative, a military hospital was installed in Schloss Oels, the property of the Crown Prince and his wife, in Silesia. Only a few weeks after the war began, Cecilia found a new residence far away from Berlin: a villa by the sea in Zoppot, West Prussia. In the following four years, she and her children lived here, mainly in summer, far removed from the protocol of the court.

In November 1918, the war was lost, the Hohenzollern had been ousted from power and the Kaiser and Crown Prince fled to the Netherlands. Around noon on 9 November, it became known in the New Palace that revolution had broken out. On 13 November, the Crown Princess was informed that her husband had gone into exile. In the meantime, the Empress had made the decision to follow her husband into banishment. When Cecilia was advised to go abroad because her life and the lives of her children would be in danger if they remained in Germany, she turned this down categorically: "If they want to murder us, they can do it in my own house". She wanted, at all costs, to protect her children from the fate of going into emigration.

However, when the financial situation became too difficult, Cecilia left Cecilienhof and moved to Oels, in Silesia. In 1921, it was planned to place the Oels estate under state control. She fought against the threatened expropriation with great courage. In March 1922, after months of tenacious negotiation, the Finance Ministry gave its approval that "the property of Oels remain in the possession of the administration of the former Crown Prince".

In the first years of the Weimar Republic, the Crown Princess became the centre and leading represen-tative of the former imperial family. She was realistic and open-minded concerning the new political situation. In the 1920s, Cecilia once again took up her charitable and social activities. Her patronage of the Queen Luisa Society, one of the largest women's societies during the Weimar Republic, remains controversial to this day. The society saw its goals and duties in the "restoration of German honour" in the wake of defeat in World War I and in educating young people have "a sense of duty and willingness to make sacrifices". After this organisation was made to conform with the Frauenwerk (Women's League) of Germany's Nazi Party, the NSDAP, in 1934, the Crown Princess withdrew into private life.

In 1941, William II died in Doorn, in the Netherlands. Cecilia was 55 years old at the time of the death of the former Kaiser and her husband now became head of the family and bore the title 'Head of the House of Hohenzollern'. If German history had taken a different turn at that time, Cecilia would have become German Empress and Queen of Prussia at the side of her husband.

In February 1945, with the Red Army approaching, Cecilia left her Potsdam residence, Cecilienhof, without being able to rescue her personal possessions from the royal past into the west of Germany. She was taken in by a family of close friends in Bad Kissingen, where two rooms in the Villa Sortier became her home. The Crown Princess had great difficulty in coming to grips with the fact that her homeland had been lost forever. One year after leaving Potsdam, she wrote to Bodo von der Marwitz, a leading member of the Johannes Order: "I still imagine being on a journey with little luggage; that is the illusion created by living in a former resort."

She found new strength in concerts given by the Bamberg Philharmonic Orchestra and in family visits. She lived separated from the Crown Prince after the end of the war, but visited him occasionally. In 1945, William moved into a small house in Hechingen, at the foot of Hohenzollern Castle. On 20 July 1951, the Crown Prince died at the age of 69. The living conditions of the Crown Princess had hardly improved since 1945. It was only in 1952 that she was able to move into a house of her own in Stuttgart which the Crown Prince had financed for his wife. However, Cecilia was not granted the possibility of enjoying her improved financial situation. The year 1953 was one with many health problems which made her appear much older than she actually was. On 6 May 1954, Germany's last Crown Princess died, at the age of 67, during a visit to Bad Kissingen. On 12 May, Cecilia was laid to rest in Hohenzollern Castle, at her husband's side.

Crown Princess Cecilia, after a 1908 painting by Caspar Ritter (1861–1923).

The Private Apartments of the Crown Prince and Princess

The private apartments of the Crown Prince and Princess are located on the upper floor of the central building. They can be reached over a monumental Danzig baroque staircase rising up from the central hall of the castle. Two doors are hidden in the dark panelling of the corridor. One is the entrance to the musicians' gallery, the other door leads to a planned elevator which, however, was never installed.

While the official rooms of the royal couple on the ground floor, with their elaborately carved neo-renaissance fireplaces, stucco ceilings and heavy window and door drapes still breathe the florid homeliness of the late nineteenth century, the rooms on the upper floor are more orientated towards comfort and functionality.

An unadorned sandstone portal leads into the private area. The Prussian and Mecklenburg coats of arms above it allude to the lord and lady of the house. The living quarters consist of nine rooms, including a large joint bedroom, two dressing rooms with adjoining baths, and a small room. Adjacent to the Crown Princess's dressing room are two walk-in wardrobes – one for each of the couple. The two dressing rooms in particular demonstrate the functional simplicity of the work of the modernist artists of the time, such us those belonging to the Deutscher Werkbund (German Work Society). The walls of these rooms are panelled with plain, unadorned wood with built-in mirrors, cabinets, bookshelves, cupboards and safes. The uniform wood panelling gives the rooms a harmonious overall impression, making the function they serve not apparent – one cannot even distinguish the doors of the room from the built-in closets. The simplicity of the rooms is put into perspective by the great value of the materials used, which was typical of the architects working with the Werkbund or Vereinigte Werkstätten (United Studios).

The two sculptures are the main figures of a table centrepiece which Adolph Amberg (1874–1913) designed for the Crown Prince's wedding. The groom is shown as an ancient warrior on his horse, the bride as Europa on the bull. The bull is also the heraldic animal of the Mecklenburgs and creates a direct connection to the Crown Princess. However, the design of this valuable centrepiece was turned down by the Imperial court because of its explicitness. It was not until three years after the royal marriage that the KPM Berlin purchased the sketches and formed the figures.

The Crown Prince's Dressing Room

The walls of the Crown Prince's dressing room are panelled with thuja wood. Thuja wood comes from the root tuber of the sandarac tree, which grows in Morocco and southern Spain. The moulding of the slightly sunken wall panels is contrasted with rosewood and the fields are of pear wood. Roomy cupboards, which were used to store the Crown Prince's underwear, are hidden behind the barely visible doors. His numerous uniforms, including that of the Danzig Royal Hussars Regiment, were stored in the walk-in wardrobe. A massive safe stood opposite the windowed wall. Here, the Kaiser's son kept his personal decorations, such as the Order of the Black Eagle, several gold and silver wristwatches and pocket watches, as well as valuable cigarette cases inlaid with sapphires and diamonds. In 1943, when air attacks on the capital of the Reich increased, the general administration of the House of Hohenzollern decided to transfer the precious Prussian royal crown from the Hohenzollern Museum in Schloss Monbijou to Cecilienhof. This valuable piece of jewellery was stored in the Crown Prince's safe. The royal crown was removed to the west of Germany only a few weeks before the Red Army marched into Potsdam.

After the Red Army had taken Schloss Cecilienhof on 26 April 1945, the rooms of the castle were inspected by a delegation of Soviet officers. During their 'tour', they discovered the locked safe in the dressing room. Seeing

Even though the castle had a modern heating system, the Crown Prince did not want to do without fireplaces – for traditional and aesthetic reasons.

that the vital key was in the prince's possession, they tried to open the safe with a sable. To do this, they were able to make use of one of the former resident's many historical swords – approximately two dozen were stored in the corridor in front of the dressing room. Their attempts proved futile. Not until 1948, and on the orders of the Soviet commandant, was the still-locked safe door welded open. It was found to contain various pocket watches and tiepins and a number of decorations belonging to the former Crown Prince.

Numerous photographs of the Crown Prince and Princess's family can be seen in the three-door glass showcase. A horseshoe, which the Crown Prince forged during his exile in the Netherlands on the island of Wieringen, is also exhibited. Precious tiepins and the clasps of medals bearing the monogram of the Crown Prince and Princess remind one of the former owners. In keeping with the taste of the period, a portrait of the Crown Prince – painted by Bernhard Zickendraht in 1932 – is placed on an easel. William is depicted wearing the uniform of his Danzig Royal Hussars Regiment.

The curtains and furniture upholstery, with their naturalistic motives, are, on the whole, original in contrast to the carpeting which, using the traditional technique, covers the surface from wall-to-wall and is fixed at the outer edges with nails.

Alongside some rare family photographs we can see several volumes of 'Gotha' in this glass showcase. The calendar of the nobility chronicles the births, weddings and deaths in princely houses and was an important work of reference for the Crown Prince.

The Crown Prince's Bathroom

The comfortable, adjoining bathroom is, on account of its size and fittings, in no way comparable with those of other Hohenzollern residences. As a rule, the first bathrooms were installed at the end of the nineteenth century in former powder rooms and provided only limited comfort. It was the Crown Prince's personal wish that his bath be made unusually large; for the first time, the heir to the throne had a bathroom in keeping with his high demands on modern living culture. In spite of the dark-blue ceramic tiles, the room, with light coming in through the wide window front, appears friendly. Both the massive washstand, made of Schupbach limestone, and the ceramic relief of a nymph, as well as all the other sanitary equipment have been preserved in their original state.

Both the dark blue tiles on the walls and the sanitary fittings are part of the original decoration of the room. They were produced in the years 1916–17 by the Villeroy & Boch company.

The Bedroom of the Crown Prince and Princess

The individual dressing rooms of the Crown Prince and his wife were connected by the large common bedroom. Very little of the original furnishing of this room – designed by Paul Ludwig Troost – has been preserved, for it was used as a music salon during the Potsdam Conference. However, the exquisite textile decoration makes the room particularly interesting. The carpeting, with its geometrical patterns of ivy tendrils and bouquets of roses on a green background, gives the impression of being a mixture between a floral meadow and a garden parterre. Blossoming twigs, bearing baskets filled with flowers, wind their way up the walls, where the partially-glazed doors are backed with green silk. This is all spanned with the azure blue hue of the ceiling, so that the room, with its floral lightness and freshness, gives the impression of a garden salon. To complement this, Troost designed furniture based on examples from the Biedermeier period. Unfortunately, only a showcase, a commode and table have been preserved. Josef Wackerle's white-bordered wood carvings on the coverings of the heating and above the doors add an additional decorative touch to the room.

A small alcove, separated from the bedroom by two glazed sliding doors, must be regarded as a curiosity. Here, it was possible for the Crown Prince to smoke his vitally important cigarettes without annoying his wife

Completely in keeping with the English way of life, there were often cosy sofas and armchairs in front of the fireplaces. As a special feature, the Crown Prince had two glazed sliding-doors installed so that he could smoke, undisturbed, in the small alcove.

Crown Princess Cecilia, painted in 1908 by Philip Alexius de László (1869–1937). This technically brilliant portrait was created during László's second sojourn in Berlin and Potsdam.

with their fumes. After the mid-1930s, it was no longer necessary for William to withdraw to his 'smoking alcove', as the couple made a spatial separation between their private spheres. After this time, William also used his dressing room as his bedroom. A particular eye-catcher is the portrait of Crown Princess Cecilia which the fashionable Hungarian artist Philip Alexius de László painted in December 1908. This energetic, three-quarter-length portrait reminiscent of eighteenth-century English portraiture shows the 22-year-old Crown Princess at the pinnacle of her beauty. She conspicuously shows the sapphire pendant on her necklace – a gift from the Crown Prince. The oil sketch 'The Baptism of Prince William', hanging above the fireplace, belongs in the series of paintings of special events in the imperial family. The sketch, by William Pape, captured the baptismal ceremony which took place in the Marble Gallery of the New Palace on 29 August 1906. The first son of the Crown Prince and Princess is held over the baptismal font by Empress Augusta Victoria; in keeping with family tradition, it was on this day that he received the name of William.

William and Cecilia's original bed has disappeared; only a sketch has been preserved. Today, the gap is filled by a bed, with unmistakable parallels to the original piece, from the estate of a well-to-do Potsdam family.

This corner cabinet belonged to the original furnishing of the room and was produced after a design by Paul Ludwig Troost (1879–1934). The wine, liqueur and champagne glasses come from the old stock of the castle.

The generosity of the concept for the Crown Prince and Princess's bedroom comes as a surprise. The rich textile decoration lends it a cheerful character. Only sketches of the original bed have been preserved so that it was necessary to include a bed, from the same period, from the estate of a Potsdam family, when refurnishing this room.

The face of the wall clock on the so-called 'upper deck' is decorated with a rose motif, giving it a cheerful touch and showing that this room belonged to the living quarters of the lady of the house.

The Crown Princess's Boxroom

The cheerful, floral atmosphere of the bedroom continues in the Crown Princess's adjoining boxroom, which leads into her dressing room. Here, narrow bars are attached at regular intervals to the wallcovering printed with roses, giving the impression that the garlands of flowers visible in between are actually attached to them. This gives the room a bower-like feeling. The white, matt-lacquer decoration of this room, which was also designed by Troost, creates a relationship with the ship's cabin below. This can be reached by a staircase and, for this reason, the room is also called the 'upper deck'. This skilful intertwinement of the individual rooms keeps the private apartments of the Crown Princess separate from the official rooms, without being too far away from them.

A small staircase leads from the 'upper deck', in front of Cecilia's dressing room, to the official living rooms of the Crown Princess on the ground floor.

The Crown Princess's birch desk was probably manufactured in Russia – her mother's homeland. The modern desk chair, in art deco style, was already part of the furnishing in her apartment in the Marble Palace.

The Crown Princess's Dressing Room

The furnishings of Cecilia's dressing room remind one of her writing room in the Villa Dippe in Danzig-Langfuhr. The room in Potsdam is brightened up by the coverings of individual wall panels with linen printed with classical scenes. This makes the room, with its floral carpet, appear lighter, more cheerful and more playful than the Crown Prince's dressing room. In this way, the decoration of the two rooms expresses the ideas of the differences between the 'male' and 'female' character prevalent at the time. The walls and furniture in the dressing room are veneered with Karelian birch. On two sides of the room, the upper border of the wall panelling is formed by a shelf, upon which porcelain is displayed – mainly from the leading Danish companies of the day: Royal Copenhagen and Bing & Gröndahl. The upholstered chair in front of the desk, as well as the oval table with foldable leaves on both sides, was already part of the furnishing of Cecilia's apartments in the Marble Palace. A mirrored door leads into the Crown Princess's bathroom; the large photograph hanging above it shows her four sons. The photograph was taken in January 1912 on the occasion of the baptism of Prince Frederick (1911–66) and originally belonged to the inventory of Schloss Oels.

The walls are veneered with Karelian birch, which gives the room a homely feeling. The swivelling bookcase was part of the original furnishing. Cecilia loved classical literature; Goethe and Schiller were her favourite writers.

The Crown Princess's safe is hidden behind an unobtrusive door next to the fireplace. The warm tones of the birchwood panelling harmonises with the antique scenes on the printed-linen wall-covering.

The Crown Princess's Bathroom

The walls of the bathroom are covered with dusky-pink-coloured ceramic tiles manufactured by Villeroy & Boch. The washstand (this was, originally, also the case of the sunken bathtub) is made of white Carrara marble. In contrast to the Crown Prince's bathroom, the lines here are sweeping and smooth. Some changes have been made to the sanitary fittings owing to the bathroom's occasional use by the Castle Hotel. This is why the original relief above the bathtub has not been preserved.

The separation of the sexes becomes especially apparent in the coloration of the bathrooms. Where dark blue was chosen for the tiles in the lord of the house's bath, the lady's is dominated by dusky pink.

Two Weeks of World History –
The Potsdam Conference of 1945

On 26 April 1945, the building was captured and occupied by Soviet troops. Seeing that no suitable location for the summit meeting of the victorious Allies could be found in the severely devastated, former capital of the Reich, possibilities for holding it outside Berlin were investigated, with the decision falling on the completely intact Cecilienhof in the New Garden. Although Potsdam had been heavily bombed during an Allied air attack on 14 April 1945, the castle, lying to the north, had been left unscathed to a great extent and fulfilled all the requirements for the consequential meeting of the 'Big Three' after their victory over Hitler's Germany. Cecilienhof also met the Soviets' requirement that it be possible to safeguard the building from all sides.

The organisational and technical preparations for the conference were placed in the hands of the support services of the Red Army under the leadership of Lieutenant General N. A. Antipenko, the deputy of the commander-in-chief. However, in addition to the Great Hall, which was to be used as the conference room, only thirty-six other rooms were put in order and newly furnished as offices for the delegation leaders. Each delegation was given a separate wing of the castle with an individual entrance. In order to accommodate the delegations, the suburb of Neu-Babelberg, with its many villas, was seized and divided into three sectors, and the streets were cordoned off with barriers.

At the end of June 1945, the American and British military inspected the conference location. Although the Americans confirmed that "the Soviet authorities have put the building and grounds into an exceptional condition", the British could not resist a certain irony: "Cecilienhof is a country house in pseudo-Tudor style with 176 rooms, the façade overblown with plaster,

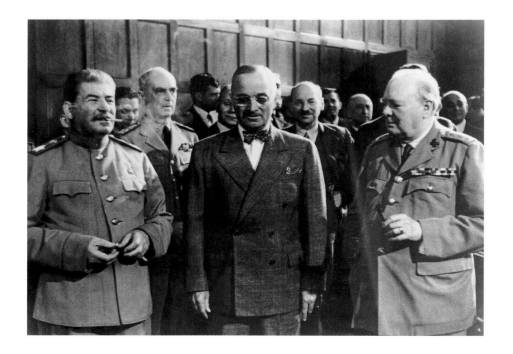

Only a handful of carefully screened photoreporters were given the possibility of capturing on film the events at the Potsdam Conference. Yevgeni Chaldei (1917–98), who was accredited by Moscow for the Potsdam Conference, took this picture in the conference hall. In addition to Stalin, Truman and Churchill, we can see, in the second row (between Stalin and Truman), Admiral William D. Leahy, Chief-of-Staff of the American president, and, (behind Truman, on the right), Clement R. Atlee, then leader of the opposition in the British House of Commons and deputy prime minister.

The flags of the 'Big Three' – the USA, Great Britain and the Soviet Union – were displayed on the conference table as well as on the walls. The American banner in the middle points out Truman's chairmanship during the conference. Its forty-eight stars stand for the number of states at the time – today there are fifty.

broken with fake Elizabethan windows and stone portals which seem to be somewhat embarrassed by the lack of moats and drawbridges. The crowning glory is a series of chimneys, some taking their inspiration from the Islamic style, some reminding one of the pillars of the baldachin in St Peters. Taken altogether, it comes closest to resembling the rooftops of Nottingham in the nineteenth century. In this unpleasant neo-Tudor place, which could have been designed by a crazy illustrator of children's books, the Russians have now brought furniture collected from all over Potsdam. Massive old-style German armchairs, decorated with carved lion heads, stand imperiously on French carpets, Murano glasses for our champagne toasts have been towered up in the glass cabinets, the walls defaced with pictures of wondrous maritime scenes and boring little pictures of village streets."

On 17 July 1945, the meeting, which was named the 'Conference of Berlin', began in Schloss Cecilienhof. American President Harry S. Truman (1884–1972), British Prime Minister Winston S. Churchill (1874–1965) and Soviet Premier and Communist Party leader Joseph Stalin (1879–1953) were the main participants. Although France was recognised as one of the victorious Allies and had taken part in the occupation of Germany, the provisional French government, under General Charles de Gaulle, was not invited to Potsdam on the grounds that France had capitulated before the foundation of the anti-Hitler coalition and had collaborated with Nazi Germany. Alongside the 'Big Three', the foreignministers James F. Byrnes (1879–1972), Anthony Eden (1897–1977) and Vyacheslav Molotov (1890–1986), as well as their deputies and the ambassadors of the respective countries, were all seated at the round table. Truman was elected permanent chairman of the committee. He had only recently succeeded President Franklin D. Roosevelt (who had died on 12 April 1945, at the age of sixty-three) and was relatively inexperienced in foreign politics.

The negotiations began at 8 a.m. with consultations in the subcommittees and continued at about 11 a.m. with the discussion of important questions by the foreign ministers. In the evening, the decision makers assembled for their round of discussions, which were interpreted simultaneously into English and Russian.

Journalists were not admitted to the conference area so that they could report on events only from the sidelines. In addition to official sessions, many conversations and social events took place in the villas in Babelsberg. There were exuberant celebrations at luncheon and dinner invitations and all parties tried to outdo each other with good things to eat and cultural activities.

On 25 July 1945, the conference was interrupted for two days because Churchill had to travel to London for the pronouncement of the results of the election to the House of Commons. The victory of the Labour Party over the Conservatives forced him to resign. Out of disappointment over the vote of his countrymen, he turned down the offer of the new premier, Clement R. Attlee (1883–1967), to return to Potsdam. After 28 July 1945, Attlee and the new foreign minister, Ernest Bevin, found themselves at the head of the British delegation, with Bevin taking over the leading role from the hesitant prime minister.

The Soviet leader had a very special position in Potsdam. After both Roosevelt and Churchill had left the triumvirate, Stalin no longer felt himself bound to any agreements and pushed through his demands uncompromisingly. In the countries of eastern Europe, which his troops had liberated, Stalin had created a *fait accompli* by bringing them under his control and installing communist governments to prevent the development of free and democratic structures. It was only over the problem of reparations that Stalin relented in favour of gaining territory by moving Poland's border westwards. In reaction to his renunciation of a fixed sum of 20 billion dollars in reparations and his agreement that each occupying power should satisfy its demands for compensation from within its own zone, the Soviet Union was awarded the territories it had conquered in the Baltic and in eastern Poland. The new German-Polish border was to be moved to the Oder and western Neisse and the former eastern German area placed under Polish administration. However, a final, internationally binding regulation was planned to be concluded at a later peace conference – which was never held. The Oder-Neisse line still marks the border between Poland and Germany and was only sanctioned in the 'Two-Plus-Four Treaty' at the time of German reunification in 1990.

Grave differences of opinion between the 'Big Three' could already be observed in the run-up to the conference. The atmosphere at the meetings was characterised by contradiction and uncertainty, which led to no conclusions being reached on several matters. However, in connection with the planned partitioning of Germany, agreement was reached to leave the country as an economic unity and to place the governmental power under the sovereignty of the Allied Control Commission in the individual occupation zones. This meant that a division was actually pre-programmed, seeing that, in the Cold War which began immediately after 1945, the conflicts between the occupying powers became increasingly serious. The foundation of two German states in 1949 and, finally, the construction of the Berlin Wall in 1961 marked the end of this fateful development, so that Germany's division must not be seen as a result of the Potsdam Conference, but as a result of the escalating political relationships following World War II.

A main aspect of the negotiations was the mutual responsibility for future global peace. The famous '4 d's' – denazification, demilitarisation, democratisation, decentralisation – formed the basis for the political and economic treatment of Germany so that there would never again be the danger of a war beginning on German territory. The Allies' intention, as proclaimed in the minutes, of "not eradicating or enslaving the German people" but "of giving them the opportunity to prepare themselves to rebuild their lives on a democratic and peaceful foundation", was meant to give the Germans the perspective of once again taking their place in the international community.

At 00.30 hours on 2 August 1945, the summit meeting ended with the signing of a 'Communiqué on the Three-Power Conference in Berlin' by Truman, Attlee and Stalin which was published in the official gazette of the Control Commission. On 7 August 1945, France declared its agreement with the substance of the minutes, with the exception of the sections dealing

Each nation had an individual entrance. The Americans and British entered the castle through the main portal, but Stalin and his staff made a detour over the terrace on the lake side.

with maintaining Germany's unity. Here, the French hoped that the Ruhr area would be placed under international control, which would have given them access to urgently-needed coal supplies. The American president's wish that the next meeting take place in Washington was not fulfilled. On the contrary: the relationship between the superpowers became increasingly difficult and blocked the path to further consultations. The vagueness of the Potsdam resolutions and their deviating interpretations had the result that the agreements made by the 'Big Three' lost their importance after a short period. In spite of that, the communiqué remained the best-known document on post-war settlement in Germany and became a part of history as the 'Potsdam Agreement'.

The large cour d'honneur of Schloss Cecilienhof, with a view of the world-famous half-timber façade over the entrance to the historical site of the Potsdam Conference. The red star in the foreground symbolises Stalin's role as host during the summit meeting of the 'Big Three' from 17 July to 2 August 1945. At this time, Potsdam was already part of the Soviet-occupied zone in Germany. The flower bed was made up of red geraniums surrounded by blue hydrangeas. It continues to be maintained as an integral part of the presentation of the house as a museum.

© 2005 Prestel Verlag, Munich · Berlin · London · New York

Front cover: Schloss Cecilienhof, view from the Jungfernsee (Maidens' Lake)
Front flap: William and Cecilia in front of Schloss Cecilienhof on the Crown Prince's 50th birthday (1932)
Inside front flap: Plan of the Neuer Garten (New Garden) park and ground plan of the palace (cartography and ground plan © SPSG, Michael Benecke)
Inside back flap: Rulers of the House of Hohenzollern, from the Great Elector Frederick William to Crown Prince William

Photographic Credits
The photographs reproduced in this volume are from the archives of the Stiftung Preussische Schlösser und Gärten Berlin-Brandenburg (photographers include: Roland Bohle, Roland Handrick and Daniel Lindner) with the exception of the following:
Bildarchiv relexa Schlosshotel Cecilienhof: pp. 32 bottom, 35 bottom
Deutsches Historisches Museum, Berlin: p. 5 bottom
© Klaus Frahm/artur: image on title page, pp. 17, 22 bottom, 23
Hagen Immel, Potsdam: back cover (right, second from top), pp. 2 (left, second and third from top), 8, 9, 10, 11, 15, 18 (bottom and right), 19, 20, 21, 22 (top), 25, 26 (right), 27 (top), 28 (right), 29, 31, 33, 36, 37, 41 (right), 46, 48, 50, 51 (bottom), 52-53, 55, 58, 59
Landesbildstelle Berlin, Fotosammlung Marta Huth: pp. 18 (top), 28 (top)
Sammlung Kirschstein: inside front flap, pp. 5 (top), 6

Prestel Verlag
Königinstrasse 9, 80539 Munich
Tel. +49 (89) 38 17 09-0, Fax (89) 38 17 09-35

Prestel Publishing Ltd.
4, Bloomsbury Place, London WC1A 2QA
Tel. +44 (020) 7323-5004, Fax (020) 7636-8004

Prestel Publishing
900 Broadway, Suite 603, New York, NY 10003
Tel. +1 (212) 995-2720, Fax (212) 995-2733
www.prestel.com

The Library of Congress Cataloguing-in-Publication data is available.
Deutsche Bibliothek holds a record of this publication in the Deutsche National-bibliografie; detailed bibliographical data can be found at: http://dnb.ddb.de

Prestel books are available worldwide. Please contact your nearest bookseller or write to one of the above addresses for information concerning your local distributor.

Translated from the German by Robert McInnes, Vienna
Copy-edited by Danko Szabó, Munich
Designed and typeset by Maja Kluy, Munich
Reproductions by LVD, Berlin
Printed and bound by Print Consult, Munich

Printed on acid-free paper

ISBN 3-7913-3548-0 (English edition)
ISBN 3-7913-3303-8 (German edition)

Wrought-iron lantern in the inner courtyard
of Cecilienhof